SONNETS TO LET

by

STEPHEN LASKEY

SONNETS TO LET

ISBN 1-905168-03-9
First Edition

Cover image Oliver Curran www.curranart.com
design Karin Skold www.karinsdrawings.freeservers.com

Published by Paula Brown trading as The People's Poet
www.thepeoplespoet.com

Printed and bound in Great Britain by The Basingstoke Press.

CONTENTS

Houses

PRESENT PERFECT

Please don't tell me the colour of your eyes,
Let me rather look but always forget.
This I can do till the blood in me dries
And not a halfpenny know of regret.
Though no man to swim seas or discover
Continents for a woman, I distance
Myself none from that audacious lover,
Transforming seams of unwieldy substance
Into indubitable gold, for your
Tasks and my labours are innocent ones,
No pawns of memory. Let me thus explore
Your eyes as long as the blood in me runs.
What I forget of you will be mere praise,
What remember blue, green or brown ablaze.

A NEW PLACE TO DWELL

Why on earth would I want to be Elvis,
Good-looking hunk with a fabulous voice
As he was, able with a mere 'well, miss'
To inform women they had no real choice?
Heartbreak Hotel is what I'd like to be,
Three minutes of bone-shaking paradise,
Not a word about setting people free,
But squeezing them into bliss like a vice.
An angel they'd call me, not one of these
Dippy types winging it in flowing robes,
But a razor-sharp boss of the weak knees,
An undisputed champ of the ear-lobes.
Stuff being Elvis though, all that madness
For twenty odd years, stuff five-star sadness.

SURPRISE PACKAGE

I was sat on a bench the other day,
Minding my own business, when a funny
Little guy stopped and asked if he could pray
For me. Thinking it a ruse for money,
I was halfway towards peevish consent,
When clasping two slender hands together,
He bade me remain silent. Not content
With that - I was about to ask whether
He or his agent had written the farce -
The man, raising himself to his full height,
Began gazing at me like a hawk. Grass,
I thought, hiding my eyes. High as a kite.
Not two minutes later, all was at sea,
I'd never seen anyone pray for me.

BENEVOLENTLY EXPENDABLE

She dreams of bringing a soldier to heel,
Putting him straight. All fantasy, of course,
No question of her hunting down a real
Trooper, of playing dead or Trojan horse,
Actually frequenting haunts soldiers deem
Safe, care-addressing embryonic trysts
To babe-parcelled destinations. The dream
Suffices her, loosening fingers and fists,
Soft flowers opening beneath white sunlight
On a shattering world, where no murder
Stems the rabid flow of force from birthright,
No mountain clocks can be set to purdah.
When her thighs part, all will be tenderness,
The brute in her tamed by more routine stress.

Stephen Laskey

BETTER FATE THAN NEVER

Sensitivity is never enough,
Should a fellow be accompanying
A woman long his lover into rough
Waters no amount of Tuscanying
Or homemaking can chart without relief.
When life blows a gale, empathy rarely
Steers as perfect a course as sweetly brief
Love letters. Losing fairly and squarely
To the graceful blandishments of insight,
A man needs a trustworthy bastion,
Something of a philosophy, one light
As verse, yet deep enough to champion.
Say, open all ports, but close the border,
Everything happens in the wrong order.

TICKET TO HIDE

When the buses of May are a long time
Coming and the whitened ground of winter
Ekes out its ticket, urban singles climb
Out of bed like roughed up snails. A splinter
Group surely exits the Land of Nod full
Of the joys, but the great majority
Of us wake to rote suffering and pull
The blankets back over our heads. City
Dwellers have always ached or sheltered best
When snatching a few minutes extra kip
On dark, frosty mornings. Remove the zest
Of kids and the snooze button cracks the whip.
Dozing alone in the cold, all but numb,
We forget that someday our bus will come.

BY ANY OTHER NAME

Sweet little bastards, flowers. A slow walk
Through the streets puts it into perspective,
How much a bunch of petals on a stalk
Means to people, and this irrespective
Of money. Starting in the posh quarters
You get the gist, lawns and sumptuous beds,
Near tenderly loved as sons and daughters.
Affected, you give quiet thanks for heads
Having eyes and noses. Apartment blocks
Are next, those with modest balconies, where
The happy sprouts rule pot and window-box,
Together a great swathe of rainbow care.
Home, a single rose greets you from hours
On the hoof. Sweet little bastards, flowers.

MIA FOX

No one has ever questioned the beauty
Of your face, how it stands out in a crowd,
Because even that would seem a snooty
Attempt to think aesthetic thoughts aloud.
As our eyes observe, does our sense of sight
Separate strands of life from those of art,
When art would unravel our souls from right,
Claiming tastes and absolutes poles apart.
Life is the beauty of your face, a prime,
Almost disarming force no one withstands,
Though petulance vex itself one last time
With arguments against your stubby hands.
Let mention be made of your lovely face,
Others acquiesce like hounds giving chase.

DISTINGUISHING CHARACTERISTICS

If I were applying for a passport
For the woman I love, I should describe
Her hair as splendid, neither long nor short,
But giving off a gorgeously good vibe.
As for the bare details of weight and height,
I should bow to the demands of data,
Though resisting the temptation to write
Perfect show me to myself a traitor.
The same could be said about date of birth,
Which in her case was clearly excellent.
The surprise is why no form feels it worth
Getting her heart defined to some extent.
With me that would need little arranging,
But governments say that hearts need changing.

FOR CAROLINA DE LA CRUZ

Like many troubled men I seldom weep,
Though my whole constitution be consumed
With sorrow. Eyes that never redden, seep
Or swell, remember love missing presumed
Dead by remaining bright above the dark.
In hell-black caverns were my regrets played
Out, distress gut-blanching enough to bark
Orders at God, grief spurning light and shade.
My eyes I left in peace, to show the world
What esteem I held you in, whose tears ran
Night and day. Within, my shadows unfurled,
Stretching, craning, ever greater their span.
As you wept, I ached until my thoughts bled,
So vengeful is true love when left unsaid.

REVENGE IS SWEET

Well-fed in spirit, one really ought cease
Advising others against overrating
The power they possess, because no piece
Of the human jigsaw so needs sating.
Starved, plenty of innocence still to shed,
We dispense our naivety like lords
Their taut largesse. The incurable dread
Of being taken for a ride drives hoards
To announce final straws to rough lovers,
Yet recant the next morning. Better be
Ceaselessly between meals, eyeing covers
Of bright cook-books in the local library.
Then the first stirrings of peckish alerts
Would prefer humble pie to just desserts.

DIDDLY DIDDLY DEE

Watering the roses, brushing the dust
Off the ivories, languidly spotting
The iron still on, polishing the bust
Of old Wolfgang Amadeus, totting
Up the phone bills, idly contemplating
The potential of the vacuum cleaner,
Raking up the past, roundly berating
The wheels of fate, rustling up a Wiener,
Wringing out the Pepsi tee-shirts, chipping
Away at the remains of the crossword,
Raising the online auction bids, dipping
Into hot paperbacks, feeding the bird,
Knocking back coffee in modest measures,
Fiddling about is one of life's pleasures.

SCION'S FICTION

Coolly dismissing the Resurrection,
Sam began his fifth novel. Warm as around
Thirty was, he felt no great affection
For weather and was often to be found
In a condition near trance in early
September. The conviction he could see
Well into the future had wrecked only
His most famous work. Few lose self-pity
Before finding true love, but as the same
Fount of wisdom so tirelessly repeats,
When in Rome put the sun cream on. No fame
Debunks eternal sway on numbered streets.
He wrote on: 'you can hardly take a knife
To a promise of everlasting life'.

READING THE FREE LEAVES

I suppose we must now foresee the time,
When our legible genes have lucent names,
And bombing the mimic but not the mime
Has mated the kings of computer games,
When mangoes abound in an Arctic clime
As freely as stains on our window frames,
And bombing the lemon but not the lime
Has riddled the holes in insurance claims,
When jargon surreal as a nursery rhyme
Predicts the demise of unconscious aims,
And bombing the doorbell but not the chime
Has warmed to the stealth of eternal flames.
The tale seems as old as fishermen's nets,
How can you trust someone with no regrets?

MY BROTHER'S BEEPER

Once upon a time there was a nightmare.
Full-bodied, murderous, opposed to sleep
As top to bottom, it roamed everywhere.
Careful to spurn no one, its midnight creep
Embraced orbit-like, customising dreams
As it went, touch-sensitive round the globe.
One night, however, weary of old themes,
It paused for breath in a bedroom wardrobe.
Nothing special, just a few chunks of pine,
Somehow the atmosphere put the nightmare
Off guard for a moment. Awake, its whine
Was almost human, a drawn, trembling blare.
All those matricides, all that vengeance, it
Suddenly seemed so wasteful, such real shit.

THE FEE NIX

They lay their souls bare in print, exotic
Creatures, plunder the seven deadly sins
For trim combinations and quixotic
Strains, then verbalise. Bracing double-chins,
One steams into a pub for a party,
Where parked at the first table, looking like
Death warmed up, is one of the least arty
People he's ever met in his life. Strike
While the iron's hot, he says to himself,
Strip the person naked as a blank page.
My soul or yours, ask their eyes? On a shelf
In the kitchen are his books on the stage.
Beads of sweat suit sweet birds of paradise,
Who raise from old ashes virtue and vice.

TANYA HIDE

Quite able to suspect it easier,
Suffering in solitude for one man
Than keeping two sweet, only queasier
Than girls who leap out of the frying pan
Into the fire for love, Tanya chases
The opposite of shadows. Tads of dark
Simply not her cup of tea, she places
Company on the scales and reads a mark
Of her own choosing. Two sugars she likes,
And a third sweetener stood in the wings,
For a man growing disconsolate spikes
A lady's drink as soon as plucks her strings.
Trussed and baked, not an ideal condition,
Just better than life above suspicion.

ANITA READER

No time lost due to none being to lose,
She adds a sentence to the erotic fiction
And checks the racing results. Pointless ruse,
Any faith in real progress, her diction
Settles for plausible effects - the soiled
Bus pass, the haunting memories, the raw
Opportunities. Short skirt, nice eyes, oiled
Seven days a week, she makes the case for
Irreplaceable heroes. For once, there
Seems a strange kind of sense in going hell
For leather - as a reader, you need spare
Thoughts to get to know a good author well.
What you lose on the stark revelations,
You gain on the sexless intimations.

Stephen Laskey

NO FOOLS OR HORSES

One of the perks of life in a foreign
Country is the expertise one acquires
In warfare. Alone among the warren
Of benefits on offer, this one fires
Back at the intellect. In all-night bars,
Delicately reared expats contemplate
Advance-column strategies, while guitars
Weep unattended. Raucous or sedate
Emigrés who left home knowing next to
Nothing about missiles posit upgrades.
Uprooted souls tire of sending text to
Surface language skills on abortive raids.
Home, bodies before television curled,
Our remotes lay siege to BBC World.

FROM FEAR TO ETERNITY

I was twenty two, the night a stranger
Put a hand on my shoulder and a gun
To my head. Young, picking up on danger
Was never my strong point. Luckily none
Of his faith in ultimatums was lost
On me, and I gave him the clarinets
Under my arm. Older, all wires crossed
With creditors over outstanding debts,
Watching threats of legal action expend
Just as much of my nervous energy
And wishing the rude demands to an end,
I offered settlement deals with near glee.
Good ultimatums bring consent in tow,
Save naming love, when I always say no.

Flats

BURSTING THE BLUE JEANS

Giving comfort to educated young
People reminds me of pounce-therapy,
Where patients celebrated or unsung
Come looking for vigorous, error-free
Assumption of their honed analyses.
Regaling the chosen guru with chalk
And cheese parents, savagely brief crises
And love-peaks unattainable, they stalk
The succour of detachment like hunters.
Bagged, it marks the onset of middle-age,
A bridge from shrewdly selected punters
To measured review of a peopled stage.
The adult starts to rule, the child to serve,
The past to resemble a yearning curve.

BUDDIES IN SCARLET

Occasionally even Holmes cocked up,
Betaking himself on wild goose chases
After lipstick stains on an emptied cup
Or reprobate brokers with red braces,
When the real culprits were busy telling
All to inspectors Hopkins and Lestrade.
But Watson, aware success was selling,
Wanted no flops casing his joint-facade.
The ripe duchess with the stiff upper lip,
Who engaged a card to unload her gilts,
Was never drawn to jump marital ship,
Nor her broker peacock enough for stilts.
The case was flat, mere Victorian loot,
The rifled duke preserved flawless repute.

BEYOND REASONABLE DOUBT

Where I see fate, you see conspiracies,
Pacts between the devil and deep bluesy
Emotions. What I call your fantasies,
You call the honed insights of a choosy
Mind. Separating smelt rats into breeds,
Your grey matter unravels news like time
Dismantling eternity. The white steeds
Of greatness you soon suspect pantomime
Horses on stage, the real actors hidden,
Once for shame, once for imperious pride.
Grotesque events you seldom doubt ridden
By horsemen lodging in rich countryside.
How on earth you fathered me must addle
Your fertile brain right out of the saddle.

FORGET THE FACE

Sniffing at American presidents,
Something of a sport in continental
Europe's capitals, brings the residents
Of the places no pleasure - the gentle
Joke, harbouring insidious reproach,
Shrinks on formal occasion, the haughty
Remark, exposing furtive an approach
To transparent debate, reveals naughty
Ideas to the neighbours. Imperatives
Of disdain only wear the trousers here,
Where delight mines pockets of sedatives,
Because fate has such an insolent rear.
When we look back in anger, we see hips,
A noble arse that launched a thousand ships.

VELVET CURTAINS

Saying, if reconciliation were
Not qualified it would be tame indeed,
For indelible scars and wounds bestir
Themselves too dangerously to be freed,
Seals a victory for unpaid arrears.
Harmony, seeking laws it cannot find
In the simple creation of new fears,
Says forgiven debts best for peace of mind,
In that mitigate truth as people do,
It pools explicitly reserved judgements.
Why men and women should settle anew
With such caution suggests experience.
Twenty times reconciled, parties menace
With savings accounts and table tennis.

MELANCHOLY ROAD

Much have I travelled in the realms of lead,
Where the price of gold is the missing link,
But once in a while have I raised my head
And supped with the gods of the demon drink.
Quite dark it is, where alchemists hold court,
Pitch as church roofs by night and petrol tanks,
Not a place for plain men to be caught short
Of whimsy, dreams or claims against the banks.
Thank Christ for the nectar, that stills regrets,
For from time to time these swamp my senses,
Knowing that life wants the hedging of bets,
Stretched safety nets and quick-mended fences.
Seekers take their chances: some end gazing
On wonder, some hacked off with trailblazing.

HAND IN HAND

You took me to the sewers of myself,
Where the width of the pipes disgruntled me.
Alone, I might have rustled up an elf
Lounging by a breathless Middle Earth sea,
So droll is fiction, but with you to lead
The way past the mere cellars, the cobwebs
And the cavorting tombs, getting a bead
On the truth was peanuts. Whether Zagreb's
Terse discos or starry French boulevards,
Caverns you found me were broad as daylight.
Never going too fast, keeping your cards
Close to your chest, you did everything right.
Then I wonder where on earth I took you,
Tides ebbing and flowing. Perhaps your zoo?

A WORD ON THE STREET

Though I would love to be writing about
Badgers, otters and other such creatures,
I was born and bred for concrete, not trout
Streams and willowy brooks. When my teachers
Praised the natural world I was nonplussed,
How cool adults with bangles and beards could
Enjoy rambling, so far it seemed from rust
And debris. What remains, tells me I should
Sometimes stop wondering why people wrong
As they feel wronged, in step by step measure
Towards mutual silence, and take a long
Walk myself through good nature for pleasure.
Perhaps a stoat would dart out and confess
To the destructive streak we all possess.

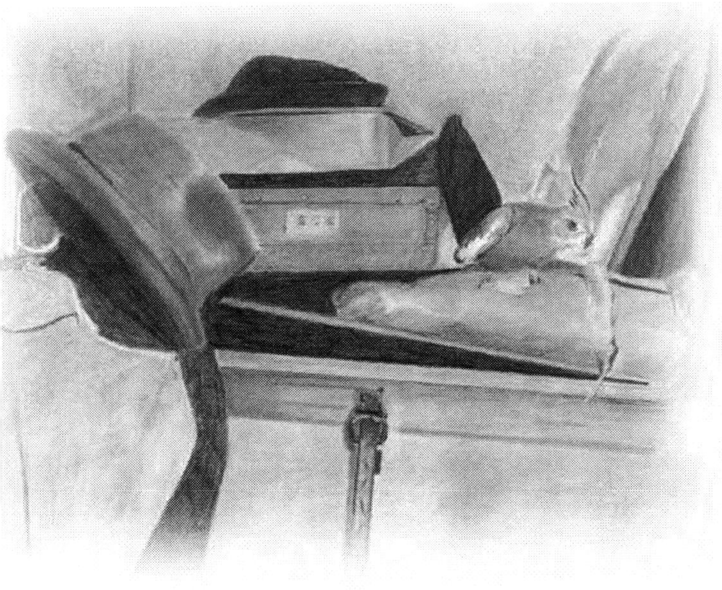

THE REUNION BALL

Few people know how many genuine
Friends they have consigned to the history
Books, though I guess a headcount would ruin
Many a tranquil soul, transistor-free
Zones like human recall drawing scant peace
From such sharp indicators as numbers.
Instead, to smooth the evidence, we grease
The wheels of time with slick, oily slumbers
Rather than let figures catch us napping.
A touch of sleep in the brain satisfies
More than our woken penchants for zapping,
Surfing and catching the worm at sunrise.
As our list of wasted friends grows longer,
So we dream of them dancing the conga.

ANJA BIJK

That I hurt you a lot seems beyond doubt,
Though you played more than a small part in that,
Letting such awesome standards for peace rout
Your better judgement. Even our first spat
Cramped you too much, that summer afternoon
We spent floating dreams at cross-purposes.
Was it because you knew peace a strange tune,
Some tell-tale heart of bread and circuses,
That your nerves rebelled for the next few days?
To flirt so much, then as harshly withdraw,
Was perhaps always to damn with faint praise,
Yet honour sense the wounds of private war.
A woman on the run from unwashed hands,
Now you will scream at nights in other lands.

ANOTHER AUTUMN

You get to fear melancholy after
A few years roaming bits of the planet,
How it peels its onions over laughter
And even joy. Perhaps we should ban it,
Whip a bill through the Houses and outlaw
The nagging hunch life a mere panoply
Of beautiful shadows, leave the soft roar
Of faithless, withdrawing waves to the sea.
Those are my blues, the cool Adriatic,
Ogled and ravished from a chartered plane,
Or the brushed Aegean, serene, Attic,
Strolled to at eight and breakfast in the rain.
No onions for me on a Grecian beach,
But milk, soft cheeses and a furry peach.

SPRING FEVER

As the early leaves appear on the trees,
So blossoms of thought on my love for you.
Light as blades of grass cast into the breeze,
They fall softly somewhere, stealing anew,
Wispy thingamabobs in castling shades,
Twisting by turns beneath your governance
Of my solitude. Soon, the squirrel raids
The same trees for food, his perfect balance
Carrying him here and there, to and fro,
All nimble grace among glistening thatches,
Beyond those prizes human minds bestow
On welcome kisses or sweet despatches.
His dashing lord tells his ponderous prince,
Many rejected truths make comebacks wince.

TIME OUT

Walking through the park, I always stop
For a look at the ducks. Given a good
Day, I get the treble up, some atop
The makeshift wooden island, a few stood
On the bank and a handful in the pond.
On a worse, I settle for the dark green
Ones, even if these rascals seem least fond
Of being watched. Perhaps a less serene
Stance would do the trick, I say, perhaps
Instead of twiddling my pocketed thumbs
I should simply feed the poor little chaps,
Ignore the rules and toss a few breadcrumbs.
Then I return to my bothersome thoughts
And cross to the public basketball courts.

A MERE SCRATCH

A year to the day since the cut was made,
Alone in his garden on Sayfan Sound,
The man looked again at the glistening blade
And buried it an inch below the ground.
Another year passed, he returned as planned,
To dig up the knife like an artless hound,
But sighing instead left the blade unscanned
And buried it a foot below the ground.
A third year complete, he began once more,
Putting spade to work as if duty-bound,
But reaching his prey he threw blade to floor
And buried it a yard below the ground.
Years later, he got six feet, all good stuff.
His mourners considered him deep enough.

PONY WEATHER

So after long winter that froze our bones,
Till they all but clanked on the way to work,
We get a springtime grey as cobblestones,
Morning upon morning of hard-boiled murk.
Where is global warming when you need it
Most, I ask myself, shrugging my shoulders,
What's become of fair play? To sleep and sit
Covered up for months like files in folders,
Dreaming of shirtsleeves and regal sunshine,
Surely deserves better than cloud this dense.
The question goes begging, wasted on wine,
Weather-girls and song, infamous expense.
Perhaps spin-kicking is the wrong sun-dance,
Gentle reader, perhaps we should all prance.

HEAD PARROT

Living abroad, the thought of going back
Home squats on your shoulder like a parrot,
Once with such gravity you almost pack,
Once too lightweight to be worth a carrot.
Only constant is the trustworthy squawk,
Complete with commas, colons and full-stops:
Tidy impressions of both dove and hawk
Round off the performance in banks and shops.
In other words, no escape from the beast,
Save humane treatment that keeps him onside,
Not so much rope as a cake gets from yeast,
But more than bugs obtain from pesticide.
Neither murdered nor pampered, the absurd
Creature might yet spawn a reticent bird.

SPINNING JENNY

Oh my beautiful darling, let me give
You my passion anew, before the snow
Begins its last fall, prefer me to live.
Oh my splendid darling, be not as slow
As idling years, forgive me my old days,
When fear and vanity confused me so.
Oh my precious darling, admit my praise,
That thrills to your voice as an age ago,
Only soft in your name and not lavish.
Oh my one true darling, ask this hollow
Enmity cease its fight to make foolish
Counterparts of us, become not my foe.
The magpie steals away from the starling,
Oh my exquisite and matchless darling.

UNREQUITED LOVE

I was never a friend of Archie Type,
Who greatly exaggerates all day long,
And once I deserted him, called him hype,
A dissolute swindler on wings of song.
Now he consorts with my genuine friends,
Who patiently nod as he speaks of loss,
The undeserved emptiness, downhill trends,
That rivet his beams like a fiery cross.
Oh, he sings like an angel, soft and light,
On matters of perilous stress and tone,
But lurking beneath rules an ageless spite,
More potent by far than a heart of stone.
Tomorrow I leave for the Cat-flap Isles,
From Archie a good seven thousand miles.

SPREE SPENDING

The glories of your house will never fade,
For its magic outweighs its broken dreams,
As its dome, tower and gay balustrade
Bless perspectives no saviour redeems.
The sorrows of your house will never melt,
For their power to shock has roots of fire,
Where crackling flames like a capacious belt
Sear enveloped earth and scorched desire.
The troubles of your house will never be
Resolved, for blasted truth knows no reply,
When coiled labyrinths unleash energy
So tremendous, and lets sleeping dogs lie.
The gateway to your house is holy smoke,
The scrawled graffiti reads 'Berlin is broke'.

RED SKY AT NIGHT

Studded with goodbyes, life could be rated
A farewell parlour. Lost hopes, finished works
And soft goodnights adorn the past, waited
On when still a gleaming future, fraught perks
Wrapping up the present. As time flies by,
Departure lounge thinking spreads from airports,
Where new arrivals confuse things and spry
Sounds of welcome disturb our ruling thoughts.
Who dares understand his first dawn his last,
Sits best on creased leather, worn parlour-seats,
Cushions gleaming brighter than in the past,
Who dares to dream dusk never falls but greets.
Suppressed judgements on life adore armchairs,
Watering holes for bombed out hello-scares.

Rooms

PRESENT SIMPLE

Let the ugly weather pursue its worst
And spit lord knows what number of vicious
Compacts, let my body remember thirst
And mourn its aches in more surreptitious
Ways than foul language coupled with longing.
Pleas for right and proper conduct arise
Best from the self, not churches ding-donging
Their message lean into overcast skies,
As love's famed argument with arrogance
Proves in exemplary form - a slender
Beast, faced with impending loss of licence
To spit thirst on thoughts otherwise tender.
Let the sun withhold its encrypted face
And honour damp remains of human grace.

NEIGHBOURS

The most beautiful woman I know loves
Nothing more than climbing into her car
And giving it some hammer. Boxing gloves
And a punch-ball keep bedroom door ajar,
The sense of feeling penned in hardly hers.
Strange, to be back in this flat, on the brink,
Snagging the reminders of long-lost spurs,
Presents, twelve-volume sets still in the pink,
A week's unwashed dishes waiting for me.
Odd, to find slip and knickers on the floor,
Tweaked cards of mine out, my favourite tea
Stood near the kettle, soon whistling uproar.
Should have moved further away, says the cat,
Nibbling the Whiskas. No doubt about that.

MISKONZEPTIONS

Three things the Germans find lousy about
Britain are the weather, prices and cars.
Show them a grey sky with a bit of clout
And they dream of Blighty - bereft of stars,
Befogged as scenes out of Edgar Wallace,
The place they concoct might as well be hell,
Where Ripper mist were of little solace.
Forking out stacks for a Bermondsey hotel
Shows them better, the sweet bird of finish
To an expected rip-off. Once in town,
They quite like being conned by the British,
Who puff cigars over cars breaking down.
It's not why you laugh, but what you laugh at,
Say Germans, motors, dosh, rain and all that.

FASCINATING RHYTHM

The accent exhibits curious traits,
To which friends in roomy banter ascribe
Palpable significance, altered states
Ever up to fascinating the tribe
Worth its salt, the manner betrays grafted
On features of noteworthy proportion.
Like snow settling on wintry soil shafted
By roots, the expatriate's absorption
Into trodden ground gets its melting pace,
Hurdles and triggers from without. Others
Identify the changes, observe a trace
Of fresh style or a new tone that smothers.
On a brief visit home no one need mope,
Who loves being under the microscope.

SENTRY BOXING

How I wish the roses thee and thou still
Treasures of our ripe vocabulary,
How envy snap-balladeers who could spill
The bile of the thought constabulary
With a stolen thy or half-plundered thine.
Instead, setting our store by you and your,
Catch-all monsters embracing anodyne
And exquisite beauty alike, we draw
Buckets from parched wells, ably abetted
By a succession of lavish forebears,
To whom we must, of course, feel indebted
Yet for our values, liberties and cares.
Generations assume, forge and discard,
One after another born to keep guard.

CHINESE WHISPERS

All the fun of the fair was had before
The bailiffs arrived, when most of the good
Times were wound up by due process of law.
Father Off, orating where had once stood
The big wheel, said to the perpetrators:
'Here was lived an illusion of true love,
The cracking likes of which liquidators
Such as yourselves will never rise above'.
Giving thanks for the shooting gallery,
He sang the praises of the moving ducks:
'Let he who forgets where his salary
Comes from be sure his philosophy sucks'.
The next day, a fan of the song-arcades
Passed by to mourn two lovely serenades.

BOSH AND PECKS

I love watching football on the telly,
Foolish as it may seem, twenty two grown
Men giving stitched up leather some welly
And testing the pits of their comfort zone.
Please learn to live with this innocent joy,
Darling, as I bring you flowers that mean
Nothing to my bristling heart, man as boy
Immune to rose, lilac and all things green.
When you mock my delight in so simple
An affair, you remind me of men who
End up sneering at every last dimple,
So soured of romance is their mental stew.
Instead, believe that what separates us
From wisdom is a mere free kick at fuss.

MARDI GRANT

A body never to be forgotten,
Is ample reward for a smitten bloke,
Tainted by subservience and rotten,
Abortive attempts to throw off the yoke,
But still in there kicking - oblivion
Counts no sin-bin for slapped humanity
Among its fields, whether Elysian
Or mined to the point of insanity.
To be still in possession of as sound
An image as politics stark naked,
Delight us as it may, exacts its pound
Of flesh from whatever we hold sacred.
The body I can never forget rose
From my bed wearing a carnival nose.

UNEMPLOYMENT

All night beeb-reaction to the breaking
Of a gorgeous scandal provides the book
Of the private morning with its raking
Appendix. Breakfast shows, cocking a snook
At progress to afternoon coherence,
Weave their tactical threads, till lunchtime
Unravels the pullovers - 'adherence
To modernity' and more such sublime
Concepts, proposes the woman who wrote
'How to survive men inside the boardroom'.
Yet the portents of a scorching day tote
Viewers to beach, woodland or cellar-loom.
Words for all seasons are no slaves to cults
Waiting to happen nor free from insults.

BRED AND BORNE

No one has ever looked at me the way
She did, contempt from the core of the earth.
After that, you never know what to say,
Though to relax you might work out the girth
Of the planet. I know women times ten
Who think life can be softened by numbers,
And none of them looks at me like a hen
Laying a table. These days, she lumbers
Past me with her eyes torn between her nose
And the wide blue yonder, which seems at least
One step forwards. Trouble is, I suppose,
You start blanking back and feeding the beast.
Then you wish there were less hocus-pocus
And something to subtract from lost focus.

THE TEST OF TIME

Growing older, I suppose most of us
Find our emotional space narrowing.
Warmth in a chance encounter on a bus
Becomes rarer, ever more harrowing
The number of enquiries we think sauce.
Thus, behind our backs, proving a better
And better ruler as time runs its course,
To nothing any great crossword-setter
Dare imagine, grows the devil we know,
Once perching lazily on fat haunches,
Once archly pretending to stem the flow
Of nonsense a wounded spirit launches.
Perhaps I will know if by choice or fate,
When I reach a hundred and ninety eight.

THE UNITED AND NATIONS

Defending a contentious action by
Means of ethics or moral principle
Reminds me of men drinking a pub dry
After dropping in for a quick tipple:
The space between the will and the best will
In the world is eating you up before
You know it. Opposing, the contras fill
Their own boots: doubtful arguments galore,
Smoothed by gravely sanctimonious tongues,
Declare power and right best together,
Not swept out of kilter by absent bungs
Or divided and ruled by the weather.
Blessed are peacemakers, likewise the meek,
Who scrape the leaves off Realpolitik.

A FISHY STORY

Despite the kind regards of well-wishers,
Not exactly known for going berserk ,
I have never expected kingfishers
To take any interest in my work.
Even the belief one such might enjoy
What I do seems rather presumptuous,
A breach of courtesies people employ
To make bird-watching less conspicuous.
Those awesome summits a student assails,
Twin peaks both of telescopic success,
Colourful gallants and nesting females,
Are far better scaled in the daily press.
Left to the muse we can scarce overlook,
Unconscious anglers use only one hook.

SHIVER

Asking yourself how despicably led
Your country would have to be, before you
Could help invading powers to embed
Their troops and ideas, is not hard to do.
The terms of the question are clear enough,
The modes of enquiry the usual breeze
Through experience and abstraction. Rough
And ready answers on a postcard, please,
But considered replies, thought to the bone,
Keep to yourself. We want none of your dark,
Horrifying visions here, where ungrown,
Tender youngsters play football in the park.
Though seasons be long as a piece of string,
Drape your cloak about me, first day of spring.

THREE FOR A POUND

Half man, half alien, Toby soon knocked
The pursuit of happiness on the head.
Instead, besotted by halves, he unlocked
Horns, perfect bedfellows like rag and red
Or fierce contraries like ban and permit.
No fifty per cents escaped his delight,
Till the man Toby, half-monk, half-hermit,
Confessing to designs on inward flight,
Sang of great dualities smelting calves
Of gold and parting seas down the middle.
Alien Toby, wrecked by going halves,
Left his own splits contained in a riddle:
What did the artist say to the tradesman,
But let sweet cash carry what carry can?

TERRIFIED

Self-righteous rage may give way to fear,
But fear takes root like a boyhood passion,
Strong and yet subtly structured as the peer
Pressure browbeating warlords of fashion.
Incremental from the start, lest birth pangs
Suffice, the symptoms first herald unease,
That of the tenant perturbed by loud bangs
On the ceiling. Then, they unleash disease,
That of the tenant scared to scratch his arse,
Lest it disturb the neighbours. Baring fangs
Keeps neither lover nor friend off the grass,
That grows regardless of cud-chewing gangs.
Rage and fear meet in the building of walls,
One side for pounding, one that never falls.

SPAM AND CHIPS

A mere dabbler in global services,
I can hardly accuse television
Of stoking up or damping furnaces
With any real degree of precision.
Idle sceptics want neither reliance
On porous data nor truck with old hat,
Though far more open to exact science
Is the speed we delete junk emails at.
One tepid glance at the sender's address
Persuades me not to alter my love-life,
One eyeful of subject-line keeps the mess
Of my finances free from greater strife.
A mere dabbler in electronic arts,
I exact my tribute from distant parts.

DREAMS ARE FREE

Much as I would love to feel possessive,
I honour you more by owning no one.
If gentle thoughts grown softly obsessive,
Far from improving on all said and done,
Render speech and deed piecemeal infertile,
Then best we have liberty from the start.
End in tears it may, freedom, but sterile
Conclusions to nerve-wracking tales apart,
It keeps emptiness within proper bounds.
Time lost to rivals, it neither pervades
With dumb suffering nor treats as grounds
For separation, save love in truth fades.
Schooling possession, however well-meant,
Serves few known joys of delicate intent.

HIDE AND SEEK

His childhood had given him good reason
To reject God, weaving such stained patterns
Into his white mind, and come the season,
The threads were snapped easily. 'All slatterns
Of truth', he judged, slipping off to confront
Real life. 'Rotten justice, no heaven there'.
It bothered him, though, calling God a stunt,
Pricked at his ageing nerves like a bomb-scare,
As time duly fleeced his freedom of thought.
'All you knocked down was an image of God',
Sang voices in his old age, 'one you bought
On the cheap and ran through all on your tod'.
Luck is the true face of childhood, chance pure,
Whose absence propels us to no known cure.

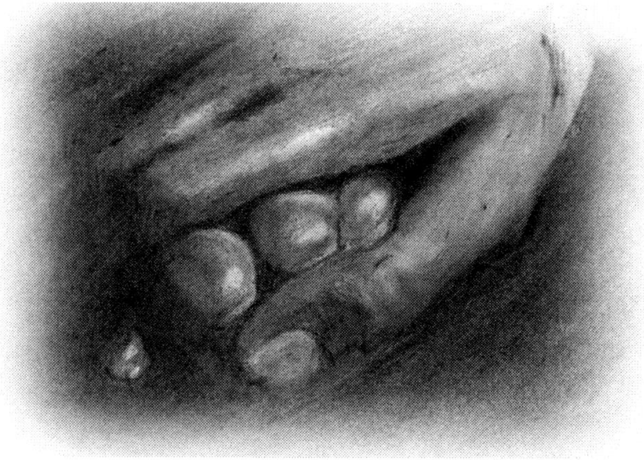

GENESISTERS

There will soon be a boom in Africa,
So fast is the money spreading. Adverts
Appear, separate wheat from chaff, slicker
Judges only. Two or three-line inserts,
They rile most readers, used now to horror
Stories. For the dark continent, read light,
Worth a flutter sometimes. Old Gomorrah
Won nothing but ill-repute there, despite
Teaching incest to a good man's daughters.
When the boom arrives, Africa will rise,
Less hung-over than Lot, no shagged snorters
Quitting the pillow, but surely more wise.
Credible myths flow, modestly it seems,
No terrain on earth inspires richer dreams.

Index

About the Author

Every journey into literature is unique. At first, impressed by this incontrovertible fact, the literary artist seeks equally unique forms. Only when this urge has been explored to a pitch of fastidious satisfaction, can he or she contemplate more traditional vessels of content. Then, freshness of mind is miraculously restored by engagement with forms honed by a thousand predecessors.

No artist knows whether this is the last post on a long road begun in outrageous audacity or the peak of an extraordinary curve. The gaze of the future pierces our every attempt to make peace with the past.

Stephen Laskey is a Londoner in Berlin, teaching business English to German students of all ages.

THE NUANCES OF PRESSURE

The lady is better company grown, sexed into
Pleasantries. Where we sit now is close, a corner
Small-nooked over drains feeding the preconditions
To a National Gallery and exciting all the world.

Duty is the dominant, tonics for tomorrow set
Aside: a ride to Chelsea, where she will enrol for
Music, course to begin next October, yet many weeks
Away, the spreading of desire requiring a deposit.

A lean man joins us at table, his portrait to
Be ready in a fortnight's time. Through the glazed
Window and high above trees shows a flag over
The palace, a flag I know not - arrived is the enemy